Copyright © 2024 Christian Life Center. All rights reserved. No part of this book may be reproduced in any manner without prior written permission from the publisher.
ISBN 979-8-218-39688-6
Ingram Spark

TAP INTO GOD'S TRUTH

The Bible stands apart from any other literary work—it consists of an entire collection of books, each written by a diverse group of people, spanning centuries. What makes the Bible truly extraordinary is that its varied human writers found inspiration from a singular divine author—God himself. When referring to the scriptures, the apostle Paul uses the term "inspired by God," which translates to "God-breathed" in Greek. That means the words of the Bible possess the potential to effect profound change and transformation in our lives. Paul goes on to help us understand that all of Scripture is "inspired by God and is profitable for teaching, for rebuking, for correcting, for training in righteousness."

In our attempt to understand who God is, discern His purposes, and grasp His truths for our lives, neglecting the Bible is not an option. In a very real sense, the Bible serves as the "instruction manual" for life. The Creator of our existence has outlined standards, plans, and purposes for us within its pages. Without studying the contents of this "instruction manual", we remain oblivious to His intentions and lack the guidance to live according to His design.

Unfortunately, many individuals don't give much effort in exploring the depths of the Bible. Sometimes, this stems from laziness or misplaced priorities, or just struggling to understand the text they are reading. Its true, the Bible can prove challenging to understand at times. And while its foundational teachings can be understood by children, numerous aspects within its pages demand additional effort and guidance.

If you want to get the most out of the Bible, you need to learn how to read and interpret it for yourself.

We hope this journal will help you do just that. This journal was created to help you get the most out of your biblical reading and study as you tap into the eternal truths God reveals to us throughout Scripture. And to help you create a plan and habit of reading the Bible on a regular basis.

KEYS FOR YOUR READING

Using the acronym **TAP**, we have created key sections in this journal to help you tap into God's truth.

Truth

In our exploration of the Bible, it's crucial to stay attuned to the main themes and essential teachings, while avoiding getting too sidetracked by secondary matters. It's like peering through a telescope to see the big picture before delving into the details with a microscope. The Bible isn't a riddle book or a coded message, so there's no need to search for intricate symbols and hidden meanings. Instead, focus on what it meant to the original readers and how those insights apply to your life today. In doing so, you unveil the timeless truths that God desires for us to grasp.

As you write in this section each day, write down the eternal truth(s) that the Holy Spirit is revealing to you from your reading.

Application

The ultimate goal of reading and studying the Bible is not to showcase theological expertise or engage in intellectual debates, but rather to apply its teachings to our everyday lives. Bible study is not about impressing others; it's about allowing God's Word to bring about a transformative impact. So, as you read the Bible, listen to the Holy Spirit attentively—and then respond with obedience. With that in mind, as we read the Scriptures, we should do it with humility and an open heart, prepared to be both challenged and changed by God's truths. An open-minded attitude is key. Let go of preconceptions, assumptions, and prior knowledge. Embrace the potential for fresh revelations each time you engage with the Bible. Its pages are a wellspring of inexhaustible truths.

As you write in this section, write down how you will obey God's eternal truth(s) and apply His word to your life.

Prayer

The Bible is a book filled with spiritual wisdom and diving into it requires a spiritual mindset. You engage in studying the Bible spiritually when your reading is partnered with prayer. This approach allows the Holy Spirit to shed light on the understanding and application of its truths in your life. So, let your reading and study be wrapped in prayer. This will let the Holy Spirit guide your exploration of the profound insights within the pages of the Bible.

And as you write in this section, write a prayer asking God to help you to live out the eternal truth you have read about.

Sabbath Days

The Sabbath is a weekly oasis in the hustle and bustle of life. It's a day set apart for rest, reflection, and connection—with both God and others. Imagine it as a divine reset button, reminding us to pause, recharge, and recalibrate our focus on what truly matters. In the rhythm of our fast-paced lives, the Sabbath acts as a steady heartbeat, offering a space for spiritual rejuvenation. It's not just a break from work but a sacred invitation to experience the richness of God's presence and delve into the truths embedded in His Word. Observing the Sabbath isn't a legalistic duty; it's a relational embrace, an intentional choice to honor God's design for our well-being and find a sanctuary of peace amidst life's demands. Embracing the Sabbath means recognizing that we're not just called to be doers but also to be dwellers in the rest God provides, ensuring our souls are nourished, inspired, and ready to obey Him in the week ahead.

On these days, reflect on the past week and write down what God has taught you and how thankful you are for it.

OVERVIEW

Acts serves as the second part of Luke's historical account. Theophilus, the recipient of Luke's work, was likely his patron, someone who financially supported Luke's research and writing of both volumes.

In his opening, Luke links it to his Gospel, calling it "the first narrative" detailing Jesus's ministry. Picking up from Jesus' ministry and teachings, Acts bridges the gap between the Gospels and the letters (Epistles) by recounting the birth and early history of the church. While the disciples anticipated an immediate restoration of the kingdom, Jesus promised the Holy Spirit would empower them to spread his message globally. This pivotal moment sets the stage for the rest of Acts, showcasing how the Holy Spirit's power ignited the church. By documenting the church's effectiveness with and without the Spirit, Acts serves as a blueprint for the present-day church. It reveals not just what the church is to be but also its potential when empowered by the Holy Spirit, showcasing the power and authority of God's kingdom at work.

As you read the book of Acts, imagine being one of the first people to follow Jesus in the 1st century. How did their community come to be? How were they empowered by their faith and the Holy Spirit? The early church offers valuable lessons. Their courage and devotion laid the groundwork for our own understanding of Jesus. We are surrounded by these "witnesses," their legacy guiding our path. Let's learn from them and follow their example.

DAY 1
ACTS 1:1-11

Context

The book of Acts begins with Luke addressing Theophilus, detailing Jesus' post-resurrection appearances and teachings to His disciples over a period of forty days. During one of these encounters, Jesus instructs them not to depart from Jerusalem but to wait for the promise of the Father, the Holy Spirit, which would empower them for their mission. As they gather on the Mount of Olives, the disciples inquire about the restoration of the kingdom to Israel, to which Jesus redirects their focus to the imminent empowerment by the Holy Spirit for global witness. As Jesus ascends to heaven, the disciples gaze upward until two men in white robes appear, affirming Jesus' return in the same manner. This event marks the conclusion of Jesus' earthly ministry and sets the stage for the disciples' role in spreading the Gospel empowered by the Holy Spirit.

TRUTH: What is the eternal truth that God is revealing to you?

____

____

____

____

____

APPLICATION: How will you apply this truth to your life?

____

____

____

____

____

PRAYER: Ask God to help you to live out this truth.

____

____

____

____

____

DAY 2

ACTS 1:12-26

Context

Following Jesus' ascension, the disciples return to Jerusalem from the Mount of Olives and gather in an upper room, along with women, including Mary the mother of Jesus, and Jesus' brothers. With about 120 people present, Peter addresses them, suggesting the need to replace Judas Iscariot, who betrayed Jesus and died. He explains that Judas' fate fulfilled prophecy, but his position among the Twelve should be filled. The group nominates two men, Barsabbas (also known as Justus) and Matthias, to potentially replace Judas. After prayer, they cast lots, and Matthias is chosen to join the eleven apostles, completing their number. This demonstrates the early church's commitment to maintaining the integrity of the apostolic ministry and preparing for the coming of the Holy Spirit, as instructed by Jesus.

TRUTH: What is the eternal truth that God is revealing to you?

______

______

______

______

______

APPLICATION: How will you apply this truth to your life?

______

______

______

______

______

PRAYER: Ask God to help you to live out this truth.

______

______

______

______

______

DAY 3
ACTS 2:1-13

Context

In Acts 2:1-13, the narrative unfolds on the day of Pentecost when the disciples are gathered together in one place. Suddenly, a sound like a rushing wind fills the house, and tongues of fire appear and rest upon each of them. They are all filled with the Holy Spirit and begin to speak in other languages, as the Spirit enables them. A diverse crowd from various regions hear the disciples speaking in their own languages about the mighty works of God. Some are amazed, while others mockingly try to explain the disciples' behavior to drunkenness. Peter stands up with the eleven apostles and addresses the crowd, explaining that what they are witnessing is the fulfillment of prophecy from the prophet Joel, signaling the outpouring of the Holy Spirit in the last days.

TRUTH: What is the eternal truth that God is revealing to you?

____

____

____

____

____

APPLICATION: How will you apply this truth to your life?

____

____

____

____

____

PRAYER: Ask God to help you to live out this truth.

____

____

____

____

____

DAY 4

ACTS 2:14-47

Context

Peter seizes the moment to address the crowd, refuting the accusation of drunkenness and boldly proclaiming the Gospel of Jesus Christ. He explains that what they are witnessing is the fulfillment of prophecy and recounts Jesus' life, death, and resurrection, affirming Him as both Lord and Messiah. Moved by Peter's words, many in the crowd repent and are baptized, resulting in about three thousand souls being added to the Kingdom that day. The believers devote themselves to the apostles' teaching, fellowship, breaking of bread, and prayer, sharing their possessions and caring for one another's needs. Signs and wonders accompany their faith, and they gather together regularly, worshiping and praising God. The early church experiences growth and favor among the people, and day by day, more individuals are added to their number as they continue to bear witness to the resurrection of Jesus Christ.

TRUTH: What is the eternal truth that God is revealing to you?

____

____

____

____

____

APPLICATION: How will you apply this truth to your life?

____

____

____

____

____

PRAYER: Ask God to help you to live out this truth.

____

____

____

____

____

DAY 5

ACTS 3:1-10

Context

Peter and John are heading to the temple at the hour of prayer when they encounter a man who has been lame from birth, begging at the temple gate called Beautiful. Upon seeing Peter and John, the man asks for alms, but they instead fix their gaze on him and Peter declares, "Silver and gold I do not have, but what I do have I give you: In the name of Jesus Christ of Nazareth, rise up and walk." Taking the man by the right hand, Peter helps him up, and immediately his feet and ankles are strengthened. With newfound strength, the man leaps up, stands, and begins to walk, praising God as he enters the temple with Peter and John. This miraculous healing astounds the onlookers, who recognize the formerly lame man and are filled with wonder and amazement at what has occurred.

TRUTH: What is the eternal truth that God is revealing to you?

____

____

____

____

____

APPLICATION: How will you apply this truth to your life?

____

____

____

____

____

PRAYER: Ask God to help you to live out this truth.

____

____

____

____

____

DAY 6
ACTS 3:11-26

Context

The miraculous healing of a lame man at the temple gate leads to a crowd gathering around Peter and John in amazement. Seizing the opportunity, Peter addresses the crowd, attributing the healing to the power of Jesus Christ whom they had crucified but who God had raised from the dead. He emphasizes that faith in Jesus is the source of the miraculous healing, urging the crowd to repent and turn to God. Peter explains that the prophets had foretold these events, including the suffering and resurrection of Christ. He invites the people to embrace Jesus as the fulfillment of God's promises to their ancestors, offering forgiveness of sins and the gift of the Holy Spirit to all who believe. Peter's message resonates with the crowd, leading many to embrace faith in Jesus as the long-awaited Messiah.

TRUTH: What is the eternal truth that God is revealing to you?

____

____

____

____

____

APPLICATION: How will you apply this truth to your life?

____

____

____

____

____

PRAYER: Ask God to help you to live out this truth.

____

____

____

____

____

DAY 7

Sabbath Day

Today marks a Rest Day. The focus is simple: rest in the presence of God. Whether it's an opportunity to catch up on the reading plan, journal reflections on your spiritual journey, or engage in concentrated prayer, the key is to spend meaningful time in God's presence. Take this day to reconnect, absorb the lessons learned, and prioritize a moment of restful communion with God.

Reflect and write about what God has taught you this past week.

DAY 8

ACTS 4:1-22

Context

Peter and John are arrested by the temple authorities for preaching about Jesus and performing a miraculous healing. The next day, they are brought before the high priest, the religious leaders, and the council, where they face interrogation. Peter, filled with the Holy Spirit, boldly proclaims the Gospel, asserting that the healing of the lame man was done in the name of Jesus Christ, whom they crucified but whom God raised from the dead. Despite the council's intimidation, Peter and John refuse to stop preaching about Jesus. Recognizing their boldness and the miraculous healing of the man, the council is unable to find grounds to punish them openly. Instead, they warn them not to speak or teach in the name of Jesus. Peter and John, however, affirm their allegiance to God and continue to proclaim Jesus as the Savior, regardless of the consequences.

TRUTH: What is the eternal truth that God is revealing to you?

____

____

____

____

____

APPLICATION: How will you apply this truth to your life?

____

____

____

____

____

PRAYER: Ask God to help you to live out this truth.

____

____

____

____

____

DAY 9

ACTS 4:23-37

Context

Peter and John return to their fellow believers after being released from the council, and they report all that had transpired, including the threats made against them. The believers respond by lifting their voices together in prayer, acknowledging God's sovereignty and expressing their confidence in His ability to grant them boldness to continue proclaiming His word. As they pray, the place is shaken, and they are filled anew with the Holy Spirit, enabling them to speak the word of God with boldness. The early church displays remarkable unity, as they share their possessions and ensure that none among them are in need. Joseph, also known as Barnabas, exemplifies this spirit of generosity by selling a field and donating the proceeds to the apostles for distribution to those in need.

TRUTH: What is the eternal truth that God is revealing to you?

____

____

____

____

____

APPLICATION: How will you apply this truth to your life?

____

____

____

____

____

PRAYER: Ask God to help you to live out this truth.

____

____

____

____

____

DAY 10

ACTS 5:1-16

Context

Ananias and Sapphira, a married couple, sell a piece of property but secretly withhold a portion of the proceeds while pretending to give the full amount to the apostles. When confronted by Peter, Ananias lies about it, and immediately he falls dead at Peter's feet, struck down by God for his dishonesty. Later, unaware of what had happened to her husband, Sapphira also lies to Peter about the proceeds from the sale, and she too falls dead upon hearing his rebuke. The fear of God falls upon the entire church and those who hear about these events. Despite this sobering incident, the early church continues to grow, and signs and wonders are performed by the apostles among the people. People bring the sick into the streets, hoping that even Peter's shadow might fall on them and they would be healed.

TRUTH: What is the eternal truth that God is revealing to you?

APPLICATION: How will you apply this truth to your life?

PRAYER: Ask God to help you to live out this truth.

DAY 11

ACTS 5:17-42

Context

The high priest and the Sadducees become greatly alarmed by the apostles' teachings and miraculous healings, so they arrest them. However, during the night, an angel of the Lord opens the prison doors, releasing the apostles, who are then instructed to go and preach in the temple. The council convenes, but when they send for the apostles, they discover that they are back in the temple teaching. Despite the council's warnings, the apostles boldly proclaim the message of Jesus as the Christ, leading to further anger among the religious leaders. Gamaliel, a respected Pharisee, advises caution, suggesting that if the apostles' work is of human origin, it will fail, but if it is of God, they will not be able to overthrow it. The council agrees, flogs the apostles, and orders them not to speak in the name of Jesus, but the apostles rejoice in their suffering for the sake of Christ and continue to teach and preach both publicly and from house to house.

TRUTH: What is the eternal truth that God is revealing to you?

____

____

____

____

____

APPLICATION: How will you apply this truth to your life?

____

____

____

____

____

PRAYER: Ask God to help you to live out this truth.

____

____

____

____

____

DAY 12
ACTS 6:1-7

Context

As the number of disciples in the early church increases, a complaint arises among the Greek-speaking Jews that their widows are being overlooked in the daily distribution of food. The apostles gather the disciples and propose selecting seven men full of the Spirit and wisdom to oversee this task, allowing the apostles to focus on prayer and the ministry of the word. The proposal is met with approval by the whole group, and they choose Stephen, Philip, Prochorus, Nicanor, Timon, Parmenas, and Nicolas to serve in this capacity. The apostles pray over them and lay hands on them, commissioning them for their service. The word of God continues to spread, and the number of disciples in Jerusalem grows rapidly, including a great many priests who come to faith in Jesus.

TRUTH: What is the eternal truth that God is revealing to you?

____

____

____

____

____

APPLICATION: How will you apply this truth to your life?

____

____

____

____

____

PRAYER: Ask God to help you to live out this truth.

____

____

____

____

____

DAY 13

ACTS 6:8-15

Context

Stephen, one of the seven chosen to oversee the distribution of food, is described as a man full of God's grace and power, performing great wonders and signs among the people. Opposition arises against him from members of the Synagogue, who argue with Stephen but are unable to withstand his wisdom and the Spirit by which he speaks. They bring false accusations against him, claiming that he speaks blasphemous words against Moses and God. Stirring up the people, they bring Stephen before the Sanhedrin, where false witnesses testify against him. Despite the accusations, Stephen's countenance appears like that of an angel as he stands before the high priest.

TRUTH: What is the eternal truth that God is revealing to you?

____

____

____

____

____

APPLICATION: How will you apply this truth to your life?

____

____

____

____

____

____

PRAYER: Ask God to help you to live out this truth.

____

____

____

____

____

____

DAY 14

Sabbath Day

Today marks a Rest Day. The focus is simple: rest in the presence of God. Whether it's an opportunity to catch up on the reading plan, journal reflections on your spiritual journey, or engage in concentrated prayer, the key is to spend meaningful time in God's presence. Take this day to reconnect, absorb the lessons learned, and prioritize a moment of restful communion with God.

Reflect and write about what God has taught you this past week.

DAY 15

ACTS 7:1-22

Context

Stephen is brought before the high priest and asked to defend himself against the accusations. In response, Stephen delivers a powerful response recounting the history of Israel, beginning with Abraham's call by God to leave his homeland and journey to a new land that God would show him. Stephen highlights key figures such as Joseph and Moses, emphasizing God's faithfulness to His promises despite Israel's repeated disobedience. He recounts Joseph's rise to power in Egypt and Moses' role as deliverer, alluding to the rejection of Moses by his own people. Stephen's message establishes the continuity of God's plan throughout Israel's history and the pattern of rejection faced by those sent by God, setting the stage for his own defense against the charges brought against him.

TRUTH: What is the eternal truth that God is revealing to you?

____

____

____

____

____

____

APPLICATION: How will you apply this truth to your life?

____

____

____

____

____

PRAYER: Ask God to help you to live out this truth.

____

____

____

____

____

____

DAY 16

ACTS 7:23-43

Context

Stephen continues his defense before the high priest and the council by recounting Moses' life, focusing on his initial rejection by the Israelites and later leadership role as appointed by God. Stephen highlights Moses' encounter with God at the burning bush, his hesitation to accept the call due to feelings of inadequacy, and God's reassurance of His presence and power. He emphasizes Moses' role as the one who would deliver Israel from bondage in Egypt and the fulfillment of God's promise to bring the people out of slavery. Stephen details the signs and wonders performed by Moses in Egypt and the wilderness, underscoring God's faithfulness to His covenant. Through his speech, Stephen connects the rejection Moses faced with the rejection of Jesus by the religious leaders, positioning himself as a defender of Jesus' messianic claims and challenging the council to reconsider their opposition to the Gospel.

TRUTH: What is the eternal truth that God is revealing to you?

____

____

____

____

____

APPLICATION: How will you apply this truth to your life?

____

____

____

____

____

PRAYER: Ask God to help you to live out this truth.

____

____

____

____

____

DAY 17

ACTS 7:44-60

Context

Stephen concludes his defense before the high priest and the council by accusing them of resisting the Holy Spirit, just as their ancestors had done. He boldly proclaims that they, like their forefathers, are guilty of betraying and murdering the Righteous One, Jesus Christ. Enraged by his words, the council members gnash their teeth at Stephen. However, Stephen, filled with the Holy Spirit, gazes into heaven and sees the glory of God, with Jesus standing at the right hand of God. He declares his vision to those present, infuriating them further. They cover their ears, rush upon him, and drive him out of the city to stone him. As they hurl stones at him, Stephen prays, asking God to receive his spirit and not to hold the sin against his attackers. Falling to his knees, he echoes Jesus' words, asking God to forgive them. Stephen peacefully succumbs to death, becoming the first Christian martyr, his faith unwavering to the end.

TRUTH: What is the eternal truth that God is revealing to you?

____

____

____

____

____

APPLICATION: How will you apply this truth to your life?

____

____

____

____

____

PRAYER: Ask God to help you to live out this truth.

____

____

____

____

____

DAY 18

ACTS 8:1-25

Context

Following Stephen's sacrifice, a great persecution arises against the church in Jerusalem, leading to the scattering of believers throughout Judea and Samaria, except for the apostles. Among those scattered is Philip, who goes to Samaria and preaches the Gospel, performing miracles and casting out unclean spirits. The Samaritans, including Simon the sorcerer, respond to Philip's preaching and are baptized. Simon is particularly impressed by the miraculous signs and desires to possess the power of the Holy Spirit, offering money to the apostles in exchange for this ability. However, Peter rebukes Simon for his heart's wrong motives, urging him to repent. Meanwhile, the apostles in Jerusalem hear of the conversion of the Samaritans and send Peter and John to pray for them to receive the Holy Spirit. Upon their arrival, they lay hands on the Samaritan believers, who receive the Holy Spirit. Simon witnesses this event and, recognizing the power of God, seeks Peter's intercession for forgiveness, recognizing his error and asking for mercy.

TRUTH: What is the eternal truth that God is revealing to you?

____

____

____

____

____

APPLICATION: How will you apply this truth to your life?

____

____

____

____

____

PRAYER: Ask God to help you to live out this truth.

____

____

____

____

____

DAY 19

Acts 8:26-40

Context

Philip is directed by an angel of the Lord to go toward the south, on the road that goes down from Jerusalem to Gaza. On his journey, he encounters an Ethiopian eunuch, a court official of Queen Candace, who is reading from the book of Isaiah. The Spirit prompts Philip to approach the eunuch's chariot, where he hears him reading aloud. Philip asks if he understands what he is reading, and the eunuch invites him to join him. Starting from the passage the eunuch is reading, Philip shares the good news about Jesus. As they continue on their journey, they come across some water, and the eunuch asks to be baptized, expressing his belief in Jesus as the Son of God. Philip baptizes him, and when they come up out of the water, the Spirit of the Lord carries Philip away, and the eunuch goes on his way rejoicing.

TRUTH: What is the eternal truth that God is revealing to you?

____

____

____

____

____

APPLICATION: How will you apply this truth to your life?

____

____

____

____

____

____

PRAYER: Ask God to help you to live out this truth.

____

____

____

____

____

____

DAY 20
ACTS 9:1-19

Context

Saul, a persecutor of the early Christians, is on his way to Damascus when suddenly a light from heaven surrounds him, and he falls to the ground. He hears a voice asking why he persecutes Jesus, to which he responds, "Who are you, Lord?" The voice identifies himself as Jesus, instructing Saul to go into the city, where he will be told what to do. Saul is left blinded by the encounter. In Damascus, a disciple named Ananias receives a vision from the Lord, who tells him to go to Saul and restore his sight. Ananias is initially hesitant, knowing of Saul's reputation, but he obeys and finds Saul, laying his hands on him and restoring his sight. Saul is filled with the Holy Spirit, and after being baptized, he begins to proclaim Jesus as the Son of God in the synagogues, shocking those who knew him previously as a persecutor of the faith.

TRUTH: What is the eternal truth that God is revealing to you?

APPLICATION: How will you apply this truth to your life?

PRAYER: Ask God to help you to live out this truth.

DAY 21

Sabbath Day

Today marks a Rest Day. The focus is simple: rest in the presence of God. Whether it's an opportunity to catch up on the reading plan, journal reflections on your spiritual journey, or engage in concentrated prayer, the key is to spend meaningful time in God's presence. Take this day to reconnect, absorb the lessons learned, and prioritize a moment of restful communion with God.

Reflect and write about what God has taught you this past week.

DAY 22

ACTS 9:20-43

Context

After his conversion, Saul immediately begins preaching about Jesus in the synagogues, astonishing those who hear him due to his previous reputation as a persecutor of the faith. Meanwhile, in Damascus, Saul confounds the Jews by proving that Jesus is the Christ. His preaching becomes so effective that the Jews plot to kill him, but Saul learns of their plan and escapes the city with the help of fellow believers. In Jerusalem, Saul tries to join the disciples, but they are afraid of him, not believing he is a disciple until Barnabas vouches for him. Saul then boldly speaks in the name of Jesus and disputes with the Hellenists, who also plot to kill him. Learning of this, the believers send Saul to Caesarea and then to Tarsus to protect him. Meanwhile, Peter heals a paralyzed man named Aeneas in Lydda, and the news of his miracle leads many to believe in the Lord. In Joppa, a disciple named Tabitha (or Dorcas) dies, but Peter raises her from the dead, leading to many conversions in the city.

TRUTH: What is the eternal truth that God is revealing to you?

____

____

____

____

____

APPLICATION: How will you apply this truth to your life?

____

____

____

____

____

PRAYER: Ask God to help you to live out this truth.

____

____

____

____

____

DAY 23

ACTS 10:1-33

Context

In Caesarea, there is a Roman centurion named Cornelius, who is devout and fears God along with his household, giving generously to the people and praying continually to God. One day, Cornelius has a vision in which an angel of God instructs him to send men to Joppa to bring back a man named Simon Peter, who is lodging with Simon, a tanner, by the sea. Meanwhile, in Joppa, Peter goes up on the roof to pray and has a vision of a sheet descending from heaven with various animals considered unclean by Jewish laws. A voice tells Peter to kill and eat, but Peter refuses, citing his adherence to Jewish customs. The voice responds by saying, "What God has made clean, do not call common." This happens three times before the sheet is taken back up to heaven. As Peter reflects on meaning of the vision, the men sent by Cornelius arrive and ask for him. The Spirit tells Peter to go with them, and he goes down to meet them, still unsure of the meaning of the vision.

TRUTH: What is the eternal truth that God is revealing to you?

____

____

____

____

____

APPLICATION: How will you apply this truth to your life?

____

____

____

____

____

PRAYER: Ask God to help you to live out this truth.

____

____

____

____

____

DAY 24

ACTS 10:34-48

Context

Upon arriving at Cornelius' house, Peter acknowledges that God shows no partiality but accepts people from every nation who fear Him and do what is right. He learns that Cornelius had been visited by an angel and invited to hear Peter's message. Peter then begins to preach the Gospel of Jesus Christ, emphasizing His role as Lord of all and the fulfillment of the prophets' testimony. As Peter speaks, the Holy Spirit falls upon all who hear the word, just as it had on the Jewish believers at Pentecost. Witnessing this, Peter baptizes Cornelius and his household, recognizing that they have received the same gift of the Holy Spirit. This event marks a significant shift in understanding for Peter and the early church, as they come to realize that the message of salvation through Jesus Christ is for all people.

TRUTH: What is the eternal truth that God is revealing to you?

____

____

____

____

____

APPLICATION: How will you apply this truth to your life?

____

____

____

____

____

PRAYER: Ask God to help you to live out this truth.

____

____

____

____

____

DAY 25

ACTS 11:1-18

Context

After Peter returns to Jerusalem from visiting Cornelius in Caesarea, some Jewish believers criticize him for associating with uncircumcised Gentiles and eating with them. Peter explains the vision he received from God and how the Holy Spirit instructed him to go to Cornelius' household. He tells them how Cornelius and his household had received the Holy Spirit just as the disciples did at Pentecost, confirming that God had granted the Gentiles salvation through Christ. Peter's testimony silences the critics, and they praise God, acknowledging that He has granted even the Gentiles salvation. This pivotal moment leads to a broader acceptance within the early church that the Gospel is meant for all people.

TRUTH: What is the eternal truth that God is revealing to you?

____

____

____

____

____

APPLICATION: How will you apply this truth to your life?

____

____

____

____

____

PRAYER: Ask God to help you to live out this truth.

____

____

____

____

____

DAY 26

ACTS 11:19-30

Context

Following the persecution in Jerusalem after Stephen's martyrdom, some of the believers who were scattered traveled to Phoenicia, Cyprus, and Antioch, preaching the word to Jews only. However, some of them, went to Antioch and began preaching the gospel to both Jews and Gentiles. The news of this reaches the church in Jerusalem, prompting them to send Barnabas to Antioch. Barnabas witnesses the grace of God at work among the believers there and encourages them to remain true to the Lord with all their hearts. Barnabas then goes to Tarsus to seek Saul and brings him back to Antioch, where they both teach the church for a year. In Antioch, the disciples are first called Christians, and during this time, prophets come from Jerusalem to Antioch, one of whom, Agabus, prophesies of a severe famine that will affect the entire Roman world. In response, the disciples in Antioch determine to send relief to the brothers living in Judea, according to their ability, which they do by sending Barnabas and Saul to deliver the contribution to the elders.

TRUTH: What is the eternal truth that God is revealing to you?

____

____

____

____

____

APPLICATION: How will you apply this truth to your life?

____

____

____

____

____

PRAYER: Ask God to help you to live out this truth.

____

____

____

____

____

DAY 27
ACTS 12:1-19

Context

King Herod Agrippa launches a violent persecution against the church, executing James, the brother of John, with the sword. Seeing that this pleases the Jewish leaders, Herod arrests Peter and imprisons him, intending to bring him to trial after the Passover. While Peter is kept in prison under heavy guard, the church earnestly prays for his release. On the night before Peter's trial, an angel of the Lord appears in the prison, miraculously freeing him from his chains and leading him past the guards to safety. Peter goes to the house of Mary, the mother of John Mark, where many believers are gathered in prayer. Knocking at the door, Peter's arrival astonishes a servant named Rhoda, who, in her excitement, forgets to open the door for him. When she finally does, the believers are amazed to see Peter standing before them. Peter instructs them to inform James and the other believers of his release, then departs to another place.

TRUTH: What is the eternal truth that God is revealing to you?

____

____

____

____

____

APPLICATION: How will you apply this truth to your life?

____

____

____

____

____

PRAYER: Ask God to help you to live out this truth.

____

____

____

____

____

DAY 28

Sabbath Day

Today marks a Rest Day. The focus is simple: rest in the presence of God. Whether it's an opportunity to catch up on the reading plan, journal reflections on your spiritual journey, or engage in concentrated prayer, the key is to spend meaningful time in God's presence. Take this day to reconnect, absorb the lessons learned, and prioritize a moment of restful communion with God.

Reflect and write about what God has taught you this past week.

DAY 29

ACTS 12:20-13:12

Context

Following Peter's miraculous escape, King Herod Agrippa, enraged by his disappearance, delivers a speech to the people of Tyre and Sidon. The people flatter Herod, declaring him to be like a god, but because he does not give glory to God, an angel of the Lord strikes him down, and he is eaten by worms and dies. Meanwhile, Barnabas and Saul return from Jerusalem to Antioch, bringing with them John Mark. While the church in Antioch is fasting and worshiping, the Holy Spirit instructs them to set apart Barnabas and Saul for the work to which He has called them. The church lays hands on them and sends them off on their first missionary journey. They sail to Cyprus and begin preaching the word of God in the synagogues of the Jews, accompanied by John Mark as their assistant. Along the way, they encounter Bar-Jesus, a Jewish sorcerer and false prophet, who tries to hinder their preaching, but Saul, also known as Paul, rebukes him, causing temporary blindness to fall upon him.

TRUTH: What is the eternal truth that God is revealing to you?

____

____

____

____

____

APPLICATION: How will you apply this truth to your life?

____

____

____

____

____

PRAYER: Ask God to help you to live out this truth.

____

____

____

____

____

____

DAY 30
ACTS 13:13-52

Context

After departing from Paphos, Paul and his companions sail to Perga in Pamphylia, where John Mark leaves them and returns to Jerusalem. From Perga, they journey to Pisidian Antioch, where they enter the synagogue on the Sabbath and are invited to speak. Paul delivers a sermon recounting the history of Israel and proclaiming Jesus as the promised Savior. Many Jews and devout converts to Judaism respond positively, asking to hear more the following Sabbath. However, the Jewish leaders become jealous and oppose Paul's message, prompting him to declare that since they reject the message of salvation, he will turn to the Gentiles. This statement elicits a mixed response, with some Gentiles rejoicing and embracing the message while others stir up persecution against Paul and Barnabas. Faced with opposition, Paul and Barnabas shake the dust off their feet and move on to Iconium, where they continue to preach the Gospel, despite encountering similar opposition from both Jews and Gentiles.

TRUTH: What is the eternal truth that God is revealing to you?

APPLICATION: How will you apply this truth to your life?

PRAYER: Ask God to help you to live out this truth.

DAY 31
ACTS 14:1-18

Context

Paul and Barnabas arrive in Iconium, where they enter the Jewish synagogue and preach the Gospel, resulting in a great number of Jews and Greeks believing. However, the unbelieving Jews stir up the Gentiles and poison their minds against the apostles. Despite the opposition, Paul and Barnabas stay in Iconium for a long time, speaking boldly and performing signs and wonders through the power of the Lord. Eventually, the city becomes divided between those who support the apostles and those who oppose them. When a plot is formed by both Gentiles and Jews to mistreat and stone them, Paul and Barnabas flee to Lystra and Derbe, cities of Lycaonia. In Lystra, they encounter a man crippled from birth, whom Paul heals. The people witnessing this miracle are astonished and proclaim that Paul and Barnabas are gods in human form, calling Barnabas Zeus and Paul Hermes. The priest of Zeus brings oxen and garlands to offer sacrifices to them, but Paul and Barnabas tear their garments, declaring they are mere men, not gods, urging the crowd to turn from idolatry to worship the living God who created heaven and earth.

TRUTH: What is the eternal truth that God is revealing to you?

____

____

____

____

____

APPLICATION: How will you apply this truth to your life?

____

____

____

____

____

PRAYER: Ask God to help you to live out this truth.

____

____

____

____

____

DAY 32

ACTS 14:19-28

Context

After the miraculous healing in Lystra, Jews from Antioch and Iconium arrive, persuading the crowds to stone Paul. Left for dead outside the city, Paul miraculously survives and, with Barnabas, travels to Derbe, where they preach the Gospel and make many disciples. From Derbe, they retrace their steps, visiting Lystra, Iconium, and Antioch, strengthening the souls of the disciples and encouraging them to remain steadfast in the faith despite persecution. They appoint elders in each church and commit them to the Lord, continuing their journey to Pisidia and Pamphylia. Arriving in Perga, they preach the word before sailing to Attalia and then returning to Antioch, where they had been entrusted to the grace of God for the work they had completed. There, they gather the church together, reporting all that God had done through them and how He had opened a door of faith to the Gentiles.

TRUTH: What is the eternal truth that God is revealing to you?

____

____

____

____

____

____

APPLICATION: How will you apply this truth to your life?

____

____

____

____

____

____

PRAYER: Ask God to help you to live out this truth.

____

____

____

____

____

DAY 33

ACTS 15:1-21

Context

A dispute arises among certain Jewish believers who come down from Judea to Antioch, teaching that Gentile converts must be circumcised and follow Jewish customs in order to be saved. Paul and Barnabas oppose this teaching, leading to much debate and discussion. The matter is brought before the apostles and elders in Jerusalem, where Peter recounts how God had shown His acceptance of the Gentiles by giving them the Holy Spirit, without requiring them to follow Jewish laws. Paul and Barnabas also share their experiences of God's work among the Gentiles. James, the brother of Jesus and a prominent leader in the Jerusalem church, proposes a solution, suggesting that they not burden the Gentile believers with unnecessary requirements but instead write to them, instructing them to abstain from things polluted by idols, from sexual immorality, from eating strangled animals, and from consuming blood, in accordance with Jewish customs and to maintain harmony between Jewish and Gentile believers. The council agrees with this decision, and they send Judas and Silas with Paul and Barnabas to deliver the letter to the Gentile churches, confirming their freedom in Christ while encouraging them to live in a manner pleasing to God.

TRUTH: What is the eternal truth that God is revealing to you?

____

____

____

____

____

APPLICATION: How will you apply this truth to your life?

____

____

____

____

____

PRAYER: Ask God to help you to live out this truth.

____

____

____

____

____

DAY 34
ACTS 15:22-41

Context

After the council reaches a decision regarding the Gentile believers, Judas and Silas, chosen as representatives, accompany Paul and Barnabas back to Antioch with a letter detailing the council's decision. Upon receiving the letter, the church in Antioch rejoices over its contents, finding encouragement in the words of the apostles and elders. However, conflict arises between Paul and Barnabas regarding whether to take John Mark on their next journey. Barnabas wants to bring him along, but Paul disagrees due to John Mark's previous departure from their company during their missionary journey. As a result, Barnabas takes John Mark and sails to Cyprus, while Paul selects Silas as his companion and travels through Syria and Cilicia, strengthening the churches along the way. Despite their differing paths, both Paul and Barnabas remain committed to their respective ministries, continuing to spread the Gospel and nurture the growth of the early church.

TRUTH: What is the eternal truth that God is revealing to you?

____

____

____

____

____

APPLICATION: How will you apply this truth to your life?

____

____

____

____

____

PRAYER: Ask God to help you to live out this truth.

____

____

____

____

____

DAY 35

Sabbath Day

Today marks a Rest Day. The focus is simple: rest in the presence of God. Whether it's an opportunity to catch up on the reading plan, journal reflections on your spiritual journey, or engage in concentrated prayer, the key is to spend meaningful time in God's presence. Take this day to reconnect, absorb the lessons learned, and prioritize a moment of restful communion with God.

Reflect and write about what God has taught you this past week.

DAY 36
ACTS 16:1-15

Context

Paul travels to Derbe and then to Lystra, where he meets a disciple named Timothy, who is well spoken of by the believers. Wanting Timothy to accompany him on his journey, Paul circumcises him because of the Jews in those places, although Timothy's father is Greek. As they travel, they deliver to the churches the decisions made by the apostles and elders in Jerusalem. The Holy Spirit prevents them from preaching in Asia, leading them to try to go to Bithynia, but again, the Spirit does not allow them. In a vision, a man from Macedonia pleads with Paul to come to Macedonia and help them. Taking this as a divine call, Paul and his companions set sail for Macedonia, arriving in Philippi. On the Sabbath, they go outside the city gate to the riverside, where they expect to find a place of prayer. There, they meet a group of women, and among them is Lydia, a seller of goods, who is receptive to Paul's message. The Lord opens Lydia's heart to respond to Paul's preaching, and she and her household are baptized.

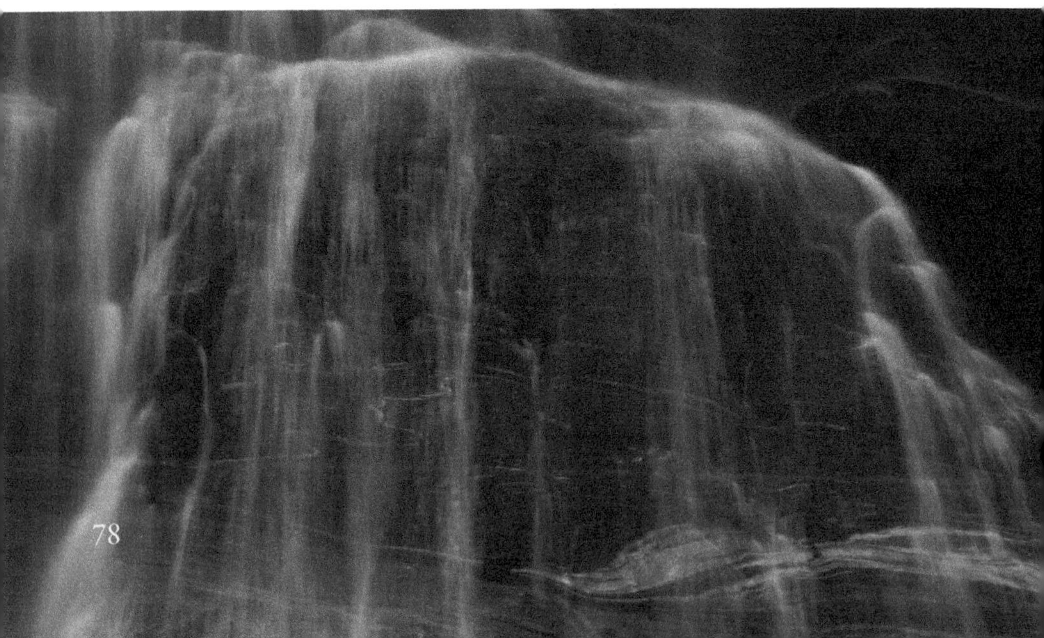

TRUTH: What is the eternal truth that God is revealing to you?

____

____

____

____

____

APPLICATION: How will you apply this truth to your life?

____

____

____

____

____

PRAYER: Ask God to help you to live out this truth.

____

____

____

____

____

DAY 37

ACTS 16:16-40

Context

While in Philippi, Paul and Silas encounter a slave girl possessed by a spirit, who brings her owners much profit through fortune-telling. Paul commands it to come out of her, causing her owners to lose their source of income. Enraged, they seize Paul and Silas, drag them to the authorities, and accuse them of disturbing the city. The authorities order them to be beaten and thrown into prison. Around midnight, while Paul and Silas are praying and singing hymns, an earthquake shakes the prison, opening all the doors and loosening everyone's chains. The jailer, fearing for his life, prepares to kill himself, but Paul assures him that they are all still there. Trembling, the jailer asks how he can be saved, and Paul and Silas proclaim the Gospel to him and his household. The jailer and his entire household believe in Jesus, and he tends to their wounds, bringing them into his house, where they share a meal and rejoice. The next day, the officials order Paul and Silas to be released, but Paul asserts his rights as a Roman citizen, causing the officials to come personally to escort them out of prison, seeking to avoid further trouble.

TRUTH: What is the eternal truth that God is revealing to you?

____

____

____

____

____

APPLICATION: How will you apply this truth to your life?

____

____

____

____

____

PRAYER: Ask God to help you to live out this truth.

____

____

____

____

____

DAY 38

ACTS 17:1-21

Context

Paul and Silas travel through Amphipolis and Apollonia, eventually arriving in Thessalonica, where they enter the synagogue and Paul reasons with the Jews, explaining and proving that the Messiah had to suffer and rise from the dead. Some of the Jews and a large number of devout Greeks believe. However, jealousy arises among the Jews who refuse to believe, and they incite a mob, causing an uproar in the city and attacking the house of Jason, where Paul and Silas are staying. Unable to find them, the mob seizes Jason and some of the believers, dragging them before the city authorities, accusing them of harboring men who have turned the world upside down and defied Caesar's decrees. Despite the chaos, Paul and Silas continue their ministry, preaching the word of God and the resurrection of Jesus Christ.

TRUTH: What is the eternal truth that God is revealing to you?

____

____

____

____

____

APPLICATION: How will you apply this truth to your life?

____

____

____

____

____

PRAYER: Ask God to help you to live out this truth.

____

____

____

____

____

DAY 39
ACTS 17:22-34

Context

While in Athens, Paul addresses the Areopagus, acknowledging the city's religious fervor and the presence of many idols. He points out an altar dedicated to an "unknown god" and uses this as a starting point to proclaim the Gospel. Paul declares that this "unknown god" is the one true God who created the world and everything in it, who does not dwell in temples made by man but is the Lord of heaven and earth. He emphasizes humanity's dependence on God for life and breath, quoting from Greek poets to support his argument. Paul then preaches about Jesus Christ, whom God raised from the dead, offering salvation to all who believe. Some mock Paul's message, while others express interest and invite him to speak further.

TRUTH: What is the eternal truth that God is revealing to you?

____

____

____

____

____

APPLICATION: How will you apply this truth to your life?

____

____

____

____

____

PRAYER: Ask God to help you to live out this truth.

____

____

____

____

____

DAY 40
ACTS 18:1-17

Context

Paul travels to Corinth, where he meets Aquila and his wife Priscilla. Paul stays and works with them. Each Sabbath, Paul reasons in the synagogue, persuading both Jews and Greeks. When Silas and Timothy arrive from Macedonia, Paul devotes himself fully to preaching, testifying to the Jews that Jesus is the Messiah. However, when the Jews oppose him, Paul shakes out his garments and declares that from then on, he will go to the Gentiles. He then goes to the house of a man named Titius Justus, who lives next door to the synagogue, where many Corinthians believe and are baptized. One night, the Lord appears to Paul in a vision, telling him not to be afraid but to speak boldly, for He is with him and no one will harm him. Despite continued opposition and a plot against him, Paul remains in Corinth, teaching the word of God among them.

TRUTH: What is the eternal truth that God is revealing to you?

APPLICATION: How will you apply this truth to your life?

PRAYER: Ask God to help you to live out this truth.

DAY 41

ACTS 18:18-28

Context

After spending a significant time in Corinth, Paul leaves and sails to Ephesus, taking Priscilla and Aquila with him. Upon arriving in Ephesus, Paul goes to the synagogue and reasons with the Jews, who ask him to stay longer, but he declines, promising to return if it is God's will. He sets sail from Ephesus and lands at Caesarea, where he greets the church and then goes up to Antioch. Meanwhile, Apollos, a learned Jew from Alexandria, arrives in Ephesus. He is well-versed in the Scriptures and speaks boldly in the synagogue. Priscilla and Aquila hear him and take him aside, explaining the way of God more accurately to him. Apollos accepts their teaching and becomes a fervent preacher.

TRUTH: What is the eternal truth that God is revealing to you?

____

____

____

____

____

APPLICATION: How will you apply this truth to your life?

____

____

____

____

____

PRAYER: Ask God to help you to live out this truth.

____

____

____

____

____

DAY 42

Sabbath Day

Today marks a Rest Day. The focus is simple: rest in the presence of God. Whether it's an opportunity to catch up on the reading plan, journal reflections on your spiritual journey, or engage in concentrated prayer, the key is to spend meaningful time in God's presence. Take this day to reconnect, absorb the lessons learned, and prioritize a moment of restful communion with God.

Reflect and write about what God has taught you this past week.

DAY 43

ACTS 19:1-20

Context

While in Ephesus, Paul encounters some disciples who had received only the baptism of John the Baptist and were unaware of the Holy Spirit. After Paul baptizes them in the name of Jesus, they receive the Holy Spirit and begin speaking in tongues and prophesying. Paul then enters the synagogue, where he reasons with the Jews for three months, preaching about the kingdom of God. However, some reject his message and become hardened, speaking evil of the Way before the multitude. Paul then separates from them, taking the disciples with him to the school of Tyrannus, where he teaches daily for two years, resulting in the Gospel spreading throughout Asia Minor. God works extraordinary miracles through Paul. Some attempt to imitate Paul's miracles by invoking the name of Jesus, but they are overpowered by an evil spirit who declares that he knows Jesus and Paul but not them. This incident causes fear to come upon the people, and many confess their false practices.

TRUTH: What is the eternal truth that God is revealing to you?

____

____

____

____

____

APPLICATION: How will you apply this truth to your life?

____

____

____

____

____

PRAYER: Ask God to help you to live out this truth.

____

____

____

____

____

____

DAY 44

ACTS 19:21-41

Context

As Paul plans to journey to Jerusalem, he sends Timothy and Erastus ahead to Macedonia while he remains in Asia Minor for a while. During this time, a great disturbance arises in Ephesus, instigated by Demetrius. He gathers fellow craftsmen and incites them against Paul, asserting that his preaching is undermining their trade and the worship of the goddess Artemis. The city is filled with confusion, and a large crowd gathers in the theater, chanting praises to Artemis. The city clerk calms the crowd, reminding them that Ephesus is known as the guardian of the temple of the great Artemis and of her image that fell from heaven. He warns against taking rash action, as there is no cause for the riot and the men brought before them have not blasphemed Artemis. He advises them to resolve their grievances through legal means and dismisses the assembly.

TRUTH: What is the eternal truth that God is revealing to you?

____

____

____

____

____

APPLICATION: How will you apply this truth to your life?

____

____

____

____

____

PRAYER: Ask God to help you to live out this truth.

____

____

____

____

____

DAY 45

ACTS 20:1-16

Context

Paul departs from Ephesus, traveling through Macedonia and encouraging the believers along the way. He eventually arrives in Greece, where he spends three months. While there, he plans to sail to Syria, but he hears of a plot by the Jews against him, so he decides to return through Macedonia. Accompanied by several companions, Paul sets sail from Philippi, following the Days of Unleavened Bread. They journey to Troas, where they stay for seven days. On the first day of the week, the disciples gather to break bread, and Paul, intending to leave the next day, preaches until midnight. During his lengthy sermon, a young man named Eutychus falls asleep and falls from the window, but Paul miraculously revives him. They then break bread and eat, and Paul continues talking until dawn, after which he departs.

TRUTH: What is the eternal truth that God is revealing to you?

____

____

____

____

____

APPLICATION: How will you apply this truth to your life?

____

____

____

____

____

PRAYER: Ask God to help you to live out this truth.

____

____

____

____

____

DAY 46
ACTS 20:17-38

Context

Paul calls for the elders of the church in Ephesus to meet him in Miletus. When they arrive, he recounts his ministry among them, emphasizing his humility, selflessness, and diligence in preaching the Gospel despite facing trials and persecution. Paul warns the elders of future hardships and of those who will rise up from within their own ranks to distort the truth and draw disciples away. He urges them to be watchful and to shepherd the flock faithfully, remembering his own example of hard work and sacrificial love. As he bids them farewell, tears flow from both Paul and the elders, knowing they will not see each other again. They pray together, and Paul departs, sorrowful yet resolved to fulfill his mission with joy, entrusting them to the care of God and His grace.

TRUTH: What is the eternal truth that God is revealing to you?

APPLICATION: How will you apply this truth to your life?

PRAYER: Ask God to help you to live out this truth.

DAY 47

ACTS 21:1-16

Context

Paul and his companions set sail from Miletus, passing through various ports along the way until they arrive at Tyre, where they spend a week with the local disciples. The disciples warn Paul not to go to Jerusalem, but he remains determined to continue his journey. Departing from Tyre, they reach Ptolemais and then journey to Caesarea, where they stay at the house of Philip. While there, Agabus, a prophet, comes from Judea and foretells that Paul will be bound and handed over to the Gentiles in Jerusalem. Despite the pleas of his companions, Paul remains resolute, declaring he is ready not only to be bound but also to die for the name of the Lord Jesus. Recognizing his resolve, his companions relent, saying, "The will of the Lord be done."

TRUTH: What is the eternal truth that God is revealing to you?

____

____

____

____

____

APPLICATION: How will you apply this truth to your life?

____

____

____

____

____

PRAYER: Ask God to help you to live out this truth.

____

____

____

____

____

DAY 48

ACTS 21:17-36

Context

Upon arriving in Jerusalem, Paul is warmly received by the brethren, and he reports to James and the elders about the conversion of the Gentiles and the work God has been doing among them. They rejoice but also express concern about the rumors circulating among the Jewish believers that Paul has been teaching Jews to forsake Moses and the customs of their ancestors. To dispel these rumors, they advise Paul to take four men and purify himself with them, showing that he still observes the law. Paul complies and enters the temple, but some Jews from Asia, upon seeing him, stir up the crowd, accusing him of defiling the temple by bringing Gentiles inside. The whole city is in an uproar, and the people seize Paul, dragging him out of the temple and attempting to kill him.

TRUTH: What is the eternal truth that God is revealing to you?

____

____

____

____

____

APPLICATION: How will you apply this truth to your life?

____

____

____

____

____

PRAYER: Ask God to help you to live out this truth.

____

____

____

____

____

DAY 49

Sabbath Day

Today marks a Rest Day. The focus is simple: rest in the presence of God. Whether it's an opportunity to catch up on the reading plan, journal reflections on your spiritual journey, or engage in concentrated prayer, the key is to spend meaningful time in God's presence. Take this day to reconnect, absorb the lessons learned, and prioritize a moment of restful communion with God.

Reflect and write about what God has taught you this past week.

DAY 50

ACTS 21:37-22:21

Context

As Paul is arrested by the Roman soldiers, he requests permission to speak to the people. Addressing them in Hebrew, he recounts his background as a Pharisee, trained under Gamaliel, and his zeal for persecuting the followers of Jesus. He describes his encounter with Jesus on the road to Damascus, where he was blinded by a great light and heard the voice of Jesus, who called him to be His witness to all people. Paul explains how Ananias restored his sight and instructed him to be baptized, washing away his sins. He then recounts how he was directed by the Lord to leave Jerusalem and go to the Gentiles, who would listen to his message. This revelation angers the crowd, as they view the Gentiles as unworthy, and they cry out for Paul's death.

TRUTH: What is the eternal truth that God is revealing to you?

______

APPLICATION: How will you apply this truth to your life?

______

PRAYER: Ask God to help you to live out this truth.

DAY 51

ACTS 22:22-23:11

Context

As Paul speaks to the crowd, declaring his commission to preach to the Gentiles, the people listen until he mentions the word "Gentiles." At this point, they erupt in anger. Their outcry prompts the commander to bring Paul to be flogged. As they prepare to interrogate him, Paul asserts his Roman citizenship, causing the commander to reconsider. The next day, the commander calls together the chief priests and the Sanhedrin to question Paul, desiring to understand the reason for the Jews' outcry against him. Paul begins his defense by asserting his integrity and his adherence to the Jewish faith, which leads to a dispute between the Pharisees and the Sadducees regarding the resurrection. Recognizing the division among his accusers, the commander orders Paul to be taken back to the barracks for his safety.

TRUTH: What is the eternal truth that God is revealing to you?

____

____

____

____

APPLICATION: How will you apply this truth to your life?

____

____

____

____

PRAYER: Ask God to help you to live out this truth.

____

____

____

____

DAY 52

ACTS 23:12-35

Context

After Paul's departure from the Sanhedrin, a group of Jews conspire to kill him, vowing not to eat or drink until they have accomplished their mission. However, Paul's nephew learns of the plot and informs the commander. Fearing for Paul's safety, the commander sends Paul, under heavy guard, to Governor Felix in Caesarea, along with a letter explaining the situation. The letter highlights Paul's Roman citizenship and the commander's intervention to prevent his death. The soldiers escort Paul safely to Antipatris, where they spend the night, and the next day, they continue their journey to Caesarea, delivering Paul to Felix. Upon reading the letter and learning that Paul is a Roman citizen, Felix agrees to hear his case once his accusers arrive. In the meantime, he orders Paul to be kept under guard in Herod's palace.

TRUTH: What is the eternal truth that God is revealing to you?

____

____

____

____

____

APPLICATION: How will you apply this truth to your life?

____

____

____

____

____

PRAYER: Ask God to help you to live out this truth.

____

____

____

____

____

DAY 53

ACTS 24:1-21

Context

The high priest Ananias and some elders, accompanied by a lawyer named Tertullus, present their case against Paul to Governor Felix, accusing him of being a troublemaker who stirs up riots among the Jews worldwide and desecrates the temple. Tertullus flatters Felix and paints Paul as a dangerous activist. When Felix gives Paul the opportunity to defend himself, Paul acknowledges Felix's fairness as a judge and begins his defense by stating that he had only returned to Jerusalem to bring charitable contributions to his people and to worship. He denies the accusations of inciting riots and desecrating the temple, affirming that he had been peacefully worshiping when the Jews seized him.

TRUTH: What is the eternal truth that God is revealing to you?

____

____

____

____

APPLICATION: How will you apply this truth to your life?

____

____

____

____

PRAYER: Ask God to help you to live out this truth.

____

____

____

____

____

DAY 54

ACTS 24:22-25:12

Context

Felix, adjourns the proceedings, promising a verdict when Lysias the commander arrives. He orders the centurion to keep Paul under guard but to allow him some freedom and to permit his friends to minister to his needs. Some days later, Felix and his wife Drusilla, send for Paul to hear him speak about faith in Christ. As Paul reasons with them about righteousness, self-control, and the judgment to come, Felix becomes frightened and sends Paul away, saying he will call for him again. Two years pass, and Felix is succeeded by Porcius Festus as governor. Upon assuming office, Festus travels to Jerusalem, where the chief priests and elders urge him to have Paul transferred to Jerusalem for trial, intending to ambush and kill him along the way. Festus declines and invites them to Caesarea, where he plans to hear Paul's case.

TRUTH: What is the eternal truth that God is revealing to you?

____

____

____

____

APPLICATION: How will you apply this truth to your life?

____

____

____

____

PRAYER: Ask God to help you to live out this truth.

____

____

____

____

DAY 55

ACTS 25:13-26:11

Context

After some days, King Agrippa and Bernice arrive in Caesarea to pay their respects to Festus. As they stay there for several days, Festus discusses Paul's case with Agrippa, explaining the circumstances surrounding Paul's imprisonment and the accusations made against him by the Jews. Festus expresses his desire to have a clear understanding of the charges against Paul to include in his report to the emperor. Consequently, Agrippa expresses his interest in hearing Paul's case, and the next day, a large audience is present in the royal hall. Paul is brought before Agrippa and Festus, and Festus presents Paul's case, emphasizing the Jewish accusations against him. Agrippa grants Paul permission to speak in his own defense, prompting Paul to recount his upbringing as a Pharisee and his previous persecution of Christians.

TRUTH: What is the eternal truth that God is revealing to you?

____

____

____

____

____

APPLICATION: How will you apply this truth to your life?

____

____

____

____

____

PRAYER: Ask God to help you to live out this truth.

____

____

____

____

____

DAY 56

Sabbath Day

Today marks a Rest Day. The focus is simple: rest in the presence of God. Whether it's an opportunity to catch up on the reading plan, journal reflections on your spiritual journey, or engage in concentrated prayer, the key is to spend meaningful time in God's presence. Take this day to reconnect, absorb the lessons learned, and prioritize a moment of restful communion with God.

Reflect and write about what God has taught you this past week.

ACTS 26:12-32

Context

Paul recounts his encounter with Jesus on the road to Damascus, describing the light that blinded him and the voice of Jesus speaking to him, revealing His divine mission for Paul to serve as a witness to what he had seen and would see. Paul testifies about his obedience, proclaiming the message of repentance and salvation to both Jews and Gentiles. Festus interrupts Paul's defense, accusing him of being out of his mind, but Paul calmly addresses Festus and King Agrippa, affirming that his words are true and reasonable. Paul then turns to Agrippa, asking if he believes the prophets, to which Agrippa responds that he almost persuaded him to become a Christian. Paul expresses his desire for Agrippa and all those present to be as he is, except for his chains. After deliberation, Agrippa and Festus agree that Paul has done nothing deserving of death or imprisonment, but since Paul has appealed to Caesar, he must be sent to Rome.

TRUTH: What is the eternal truth that God is revealing to you?

____

____

____

____

____

APPLICATION: How will you apply this truth to your life?

____

____

____

____

____

PRAYER: Ask God to help you to live out this truth.

____

____

____

____

____

DAY 58

ACTS 27:1-12

Context

As Paul and other prisoners prepare to sail to Rome, they board a ship at Caesarea bound for various ports along the coast of Asia Minor. Julius, a centurion of the Augustan Cohort, treats Paul kindly and allows him to visit his friends in Sidon. Departing from Sidon, they encounter strong headwinds and sail close to the coast of Cyprus, seeking shelter. The winds prevent them from continuing their journey, so they sail under the shelter of Cyprus, passing to the south of Cilicia and Pamphylia. Arriving in Myra, they board a ship sailing to Italy, but due to the slow progress caused by unfavorable winds, they transfer to another ship bound for Rome.

TRUTH: What is the eternal truth that God is revealing to you?

____

____

____

____

____

APPLICATION: How will you apply this truth to your life?

____

____

____

____

____

PRAYER: Ask God to help you to live out this truth.

____

____

____

____

____

DAY 59
ACTS 27:13-38

Context

As they sail on, an intense wind called the northeaster strikes, driving the ship off course and eventually into the open sea. The crew struggles to control the boat, fearing they will run aground on the Syrtis sands. They take measures to secure the ship, undergirding it with cables and lowering the sea anchor to stabilize it. In desperation, they begin to abandon cargo to lighten the load. With no end in sight to the storm, Paul addresses the crew and passengers, urging them to take heart and assuring them that no lives will be lost if they remain aboard the ship. He recounts a vision, in which God promised to spare the lives of all on board, but the ship would be lost. Encouraged by Paul's words, they continue to endure the storm.

TRUTH: What is the eternal truth that God is revealing to you?

____

____

____

____

APPLICATION: How will you apply this truth to your life?

____

____

____

____

PRAYER: Ask God to help you to live out this truth.

____

____

____

____

____

____

DAY 60

ACTS 27:39-28:10

Context

After enduring the storm for many days, they finally spot land and attempt to bring the ship on the shore of an island. They cast off the anchors and leave the ship to be driven onto the rocks, where it breaks apart. By God's grace, everyone reaches shore safely, some on planks and others on pieces of the ship. They find themselves on the island of Malta, where the native people show them unusual kindness, building a fire to warm them in the rain. As Paul gathers sticks for the fire, a snake latches onto his hand, but he shakes it off into the fire without harm. The islanders expect him to swell up or suddenly fall dead, but when he shows no ill effects, they regard him as a god. Paul then heals Publius' father and others on the island who were sick, leading to the islanders showing them great honor and providing for their needs. After three months, they sail on to Rome aboard another ship from Alexandria.

TRUTH: What is the eternal truth that God is revealing to you?

____

____

____

____

____

APPLICATION: How will you apply this truth to your life?

____

____

____

____

____

PRAYER: Ask God to help you to live out this truth.

____

____

____

____

____

DAY 61

ACTS 28:11-31

Context

As we conclude our journey through Acts, we find Paul reaching Rome, and he is allowed to live by himself with a soldier guarding him. Three days later, he calls together the leaders of the Jews and explains his situation, expressing his innocence and willingness to preach the Gospel to them. Though some believe and others do not, they agree to meet with Paul again to hear more. Paul continues to preach to all who come to him, testifying about the kingdom of God and persuading them about Jesus, using the Law of Moses and the Prophets. He spends two years in his own rented house, welcoming all who come to him, boldly and unhindered, preaching the kingdom of God and teaching about the Lord Jesus Christ.

TRUTH: What is the eternal truth that God is revealing to you?

____

____

____

____

____

APPLICATION: How will you apply this truth to your life?

____

____

____

____

____

PRAYER: Ask God to help you to live out this truth.

____

____

____

____

____

DAY 62

Sabbath Day

Today marks a Rest Day. The focus is simple: rest in the presence of God. Whether it's an opportunity to catch up on the reading plan, journal reflections on your spiritual journey, or engage in concentrated prayer, the key is to spend meaningful time in God's presence. Take this day to reconnect, absorb the lessons learned, and prioritize a moment of restful communion with God.

Reflect and write about what God has taught you this past week.

www.ingramcontent.com/pod-product-compliance
Lightning Source LLC
Chambersburg PA
CBHW042047150726
48005CB00034B/2212